Poetry in Stitches

2

Edited by
Linda Connell
&
Con Connell

National Needlework Archive

Dedication

*To Ma: For instilling the love of learning
and creativity in the whole family*

Front Cover details from: **Windy nights, The Dandelion, Valentine
Tree Prayer, The Pig, An Otter**

Back Cover detail from: **Tea**

First published in the United Kingdom in 2008 by
The National Needlework Archive
Boldre House, 5 Boldrewood Road
Southampton, Hampshire, SO16 7BW
Registered Charity No. 1109930
www.nationalneedleworkarchive.org.uk

Poetry in Stitches 2 © Linda Connell & Con Connell 2008
Text © Linda Connell & Con Connell
Photographs: Andy Brown, Romsey, Hampshire © NNA

Artwork and print by
Solent Design Studio Ltd
Claylands Road, Bishops Waltham
Hampshire SO32 1BH

British Library Cataloguing in Publication Data
A catalogue record for this book is available from the British Library

ISBN   978 0 9550790 2 3

Contents

Poetry in Stitches is a community art project launched by The National Needlework Archive in 2004 in association with Poems in the Waiting Room. The aim of the project is to combine the two important cultural media of textile art and poetry, present them in a format which allows a new perception of each in relation to the other, and to display them together in a public art arena.
Poetry in Stitches 2 is the second phase of the project, and was launched in 2007.

The National Needlework Archive (NNA) operates primarily to document, photograph and archive information about textile artefacts of all types and ages, which are housed in the community throughout Britain. As well as work in public buildings, offices, schools, etc., the NNA records work belonging to organisations and clubs, and facilitates the cataloguing of private collections. The NNA archives include *The National Record of Millennium Needlework, The National Federation of Women's Institutes' Textile Archive* and *The National Kneeler Database*. The NNA also promotes new work for public display, aids textile education and research, and houses books, textiles and textile-related artefacts for public access.
The NNA was established in 1999 and is Registered Charity No.1109930

Poems in the Waiting Room (PitWR) is a nationwide arts in health registered charity (No. 1099033) providing free poetry cards for patients in health service waiting rooms. Patients are invited to keep the cards, and over half a million copies of *Poems in the Waiting Room* have been taken by patients since 1998. The objective of the charity is to promote poetry, to make a patient's wait more pleasant, and to show appreciation of the health services. The charity is funded by private trusts and a Friends scheme.

**This publication has been made possible through the help of a generous grant from:-
The Beatrice Trust**

The Beatrice Trust was established by the family of the Editor of Poems in the Waiting Room. It has the objectives of supporting poetry, and of aiding charities caring for children with severe disabilities. The Beatrice Trust has been the principal funding source for Poems in the Waiting Room since its foundation in 1996.

Acknowledgements

The *National Needlework Archive* wishes to thank the following for permission to reprint copyright material.

Moniza Alvi 'Arrival 1946' from *Split World: Poems 1990 – 2005* published by Bloodaxe Books 2008 ©Moniza Alvi, reprinted by permission of Bloodaxe Books. **Elizabeth Bewick** 'A Day by the Sea' from *Heartsease* ©Elizabeth Bewick 1991, reproduced by permission of Peterloo Poets. **Ann Bonner** 'On Midsummer's Eve' from *Let's Celebrate Festival Poems*, OUP 1997, ©Ann Bonner, reprinted by permission of the author. **Laurence Binyon** 'The Little Dancers', reprinted by permission of the Society of Authors as the Literary Representative of the Estate of Laurence Binyon. **Con Connell** 'Love in a Cold Climate' from *'The Saint'* 2008, 'The Vanishing Zebra' and 'Enigma' ©Con Connell 2008, reprinted by permission of the author. **E. E. Cummings** 'i carry your heart with me(I carry it in' is reprinted from *Complete Poems 1904-1962* by E.E. Cummings, edited by George J. Firmage, by permission of W.W. Norton & Company. Copyright © 1991 by the Trustees for the E.E. Cummings Trust and George James Firmage. **W.H. Davies** 'For Sale' from *Selected Poems* published by OUP 1985 ©W.H. Davies, reprinted by permission of Dee & Griffin, Trustees for the Estate of W.H. Davies. **Carol Ann Duffy** 'Tea' from *Rapture*, published by Picador 2006 & 'Valentine' from *Mean Time*, published by Anvil Press 1993, ©Carol Ann Duffy, reprinted by permission of the author. **Harriet Green** 'The Cello Player', from Luciana: *Below the Belt* ©Harriet Green, published by Chameleon Library 2004, reprinted by permission of the author. **Alma Lusby Harding** 'A New Home for Saxons' from *A Garden of Bright Images*, published 1993, reprinted by permission of the author. **Ted Hughes** 'Dragonfly' and 'The Otter', from *Collected Poems*, ©Ted Hughes, reproduced by permission of Faber and Faber. **Jenny Joseph** 'The sun has burst the sky' from *Selected Poems*, published by Bloodaxe Books, 1992 ©Jenny Joseph, reprinted by permission of the author. **Roger McGough** 'Reward and Punishment', from *Good Enough to Eat*, published by Penguin Books 2002, reprinted by permission of the author. **Spike Milligan** 'On the Ning Nang Nong' from *Complete Poems* published by Michael Joseph 1997 ©Spike Milligan, reprinted by permission of Spike Milligan Productions Ltd. **Pat Moon** 'Today's Tomorrow' from *Green Poems*, reprinted by permission of the author. **Matt Nunn** 'Doing the Big Bang Theory, from *Happy 'cos I'm Blue* published by Heaventree Press 2006, ©Matt Nunn, reprinted by permission of the author. **James Reeves** 'The Snail' from *Complete Poems for Children (Heinemann)* ©James Reeves, reprinted by permission of Laura Cecil Literary Agency on behalf of the James Reeves Estate. **Christopher Reid** 'A Tent', from *All Sorts* published by Ondt and Gracehopper 1999 ©Christopher Reid, reprinted by permission of the author. **Louisa Saunders** 'A Picturesque Dream in Goathland' from *Rhyme versus Reason* published by Poetry in Print 2001 ©Louisa Saunders, reprinted by permission of the author. **Richard Stewart** 'In Memoriam : October 16th 1987' from *Eastern Poets* published by Arrival Press 1992 and 'River Deben', from *Poetry Cornwall* published by Palores Publications 2008 ©Richard Stewart, reprinted by permission of the author. **W.B. Yeats** 'The Cat and the Moon' and 'The Lake Isle of Innisfree' from *The Collected Poems of W.B.Yeats*, reprinted by permission of A.P. Watt Ltd on behalf of Grainne Yeats.

We are grateful to the following, whose work was previously published in *Poems in the Waiting Room*, for permission to reprint their work here.
Ruth Fainlight 'Handbag' ©Ruth Fainlight, reprinted by permission of the author. **Daphne Schiller** 'Doormat' ©Daphne Schiller, reprinted by permission of the author. **Christopher Daniel** 'The Dandelion: Nature's Sundial' ©Christopher Daniel, reprinted by permission of the author. **Eve Jackson** 'Joy' ©Eve Jackson, reprinted by permission of the author.

We also thank the following authors, whose work is published here for the first time, and whose poems are reprinted by permission of the author. **Dawn Ashcroft** 'Windmills of the Night' ©Dawn Ashcroft 2008; **Margaret Crosfield** 'Abbey Ruins' ©Margaret Crosfield; **Sue Flawn** 'Seascapes' ©Sue Flawn; **Pauline Hand** 'There's a Poem Hiding in Wan's Fish and Chip Shop' ©Pauline Hand; **Gillian Wright** 'The Story of Creation' ©Gillian Wright.

Anyone wishing to take part in **Poetry in Stitches**, either as a textile artist, poet, or as a host to a Poetry in Stitches picture or exhibition, should see the NNA web site www.nationalneedleworkarchive.org.uk, or contact the NNA *(address at front of book)*.

Introduction

When the National Needlework Archive published the first *'Poetry in Stitches'* in 2005, we could hardly have anticipated its popularity. The idea of combining textile art and poetry, side by side, so that each complemented the other, was something that we had felt sure would benefit each medium and in the end we were overwhelmed by the sheer volume of the unerringly positive reactions we received from everyone in response to this concept.

As the exhibition of the entire collection toured the country, and later as smaller selections were placed in health service and other locations, hundreds of appreciative people contacted us to say how wonderfully inspiring they had found the project. And a constantly-asked question was always 'When are you going to do it again?'

Because an important part of the NNA's remit is to encourage (as well as archive) community-based textile art projects, we needed little encouragement to respond to all those imploring us to start 'Poetry in Stitches 2'. Together with our partners, PitWR, we launched Poetry in Stitches 2 in 2007, and this catalogue complements the nationwide exhibitions that give as many members of the public as possible an opportunity to enjoy the resulting new pictures and poems.

As with the original Poetry in Stitches, we produced a booklet of poems as a basis for visual ideas, but we allowed the textile artists to choose poems other than these if they wished. The artists could choose poems that meant something to them personally, either in terms of memory or emotion, or ones which inspired a particularly vivid mental image for their picture. There was one exception to this free choice. None of the poems chosen previously for Poetry in Stitches could be used again for Poetry in Stitches 2, thus ensuring that we did our best to encourage fresh inspiration and greater variety. Our textile artists did not disappoint us with their choices. Once again we have a very wide range of poetry, ancient and modern, familiar and unfamiliar.

As before, the range of poems chosen presented us, as editors, a challenge in compiling this catalogue. After much careful consideration, six themes seemed to emerge from the poems. Many of the artists found that **A Sense of Place** inspired them, either in a light-hearted way or more reflectively. The natural world is well represented and we have collected these poems together into a selection entitled **The Touch of Nature**. So much poetry comes from the heart it was not surprising that some felt themselves moved by **Words of Love**, with the intimacy and warmth of romance, while many of the poems included in **Spiritual Reflections** reveal a more contemplative mood. A sombre tone emerges in some of the poems in **Backward Glances**, replete with memories and reminiscences. However, this mood lightens and we finish with a selection of poems conveying a sense of fun and joy, sometimes even silliness, to be found in **Young at Heart**.

We hope that you enjoy Poetry in Stitches 2, either through the poems or the textile art, but best of all, through the combination of the two.

1   **ISCA Tatters**
    Tatting on painted canvas

For Sale

Four hundred years this little house has stood
Through wind and fire, through earthquake and through flood;
Still its old beams, though bulged and warped, are strong,
In spite of gaping wounds both deep and long.
The doors are low and give such narrow space
We must walk humbly in this place.
The windows here, no longer square or straight,
Are able now, from fantastic state,
To squint down their own walls, and see the flowers
That get more drippings from the eaves than showers.
Six hundred pounds for this precious stone!
These little, quaint old windows squinting down;
This orchard, with its apples' last appeal
To dumping or sweet cider; this deep well,
Whose little eye has sparkled from its birth -
Four hundred years in sixty feet of earth!

W.H. Davies (1871 – 1940)

A Sense of Place

"And I shall have some peace there..."

W.B. Yeats

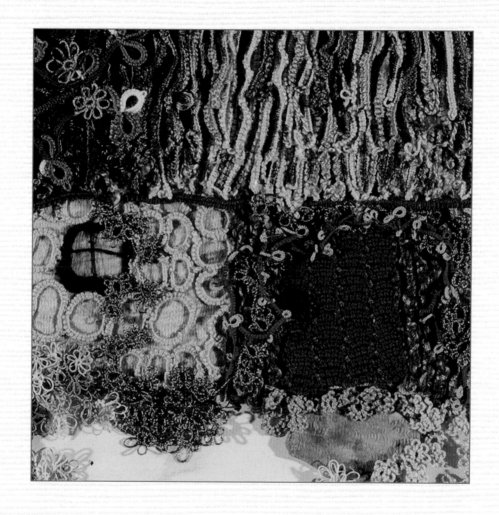

Centuries of stone, bricks and landscape echo through the poems chosen for this section, as we are treated to images of ancient ruins or mental snapshots of scenic locations, together with some reflections of everyday places that have struck a chord with both poet and artist.

Abbey Ruins

Abbey in ruins and falling apart
Gave hand to the artisans expressing
                    their art,
Beauty in buildings so old and well worn
Revealing, beguiling and eerie at dawn.
Mystical, wondrous, builders of old
Have handed us beauty brave and so bold.
The skills of their labours tried and
                    well honed,
A legacy left to enjoy and behold.

Margaret Crosfield (1940 -   )

2   **Margaret Crosfield**
*Bonding, overlaying and cut work with free machine embroidery
on dyed and painted silk*

A New Home for Saxons

A wind wailed wildly
Across slated, stagnant skies,
Woden loosed a lance
That cleaved the canopy,
The heat of his bowstring
Thundered and waves
Lavishly licked the keel of the craft
As she rode the pounding teeth of the tide.

We strove through the storm
And flew, full ready for flight,
Against the Britons' bright-barbed blows.
Gliding on, a grove of glittering,
Surging spears, striking to gain
A home to house the hungry,
To farm where the sea
Does not swallow the shore.

We built in the bountiful brushwood.
Made as before, a Meadhall;
Like travellers, told old tales of horrors,
Round the hearth huddled, hardly daring
To least sight into cold corners
Where monsters might merge in the mist.
We set up a settlement, calling it
Sigglesthorne, home for Sigmund.

Alma Lusby (m.Harding) (1945 -   )

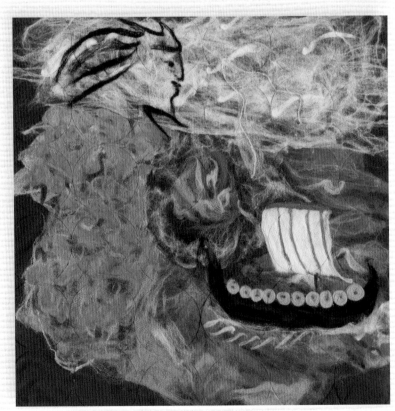

3   **Alma Harding**
Needle-punched fabric over fleece

4   Anne-Marie Stewart
Machine appliqué and quilting on fabric-painted background

River Deben

This full flood of salt water holds sound,
Magnifies it, transmits the excited voices
Of people on a boat trip, sailing smoothly
Below the raised burial mounds of Sutton Hoo
And beyond the wind singing in the mast
Is the sound of a muntjac barking,
An alien call, that even Lord Raedwald,
The Great High King of All The English,
With all his power could not have summoned.

Richard Stewart (1945 -   )

Home Thoughts, from Abroad

O, to be in England
Now that April's there,
And whoever wakes in England
Sees, some morning, unaware,
That the lowest boughs and the brushwood sheaf
Round the elm-tree bole are in tiny leaf,
While the chaffinch sings on the orchard bough
In England - now!

And after April, when May follows,
And the whitethroat builds, and all the swallows!
Hark, where my blossom'd pear-tree in the hedge
Leans to the field and scatters on the clover
Blossoms and dewdrops - at the bent spray's edge -
That's the wise thrush; he sings each song twice over,
Lest you should think he never could recapture
The first fine careless rapture!
And though the fields look rough with hoary dew,
All will be gay when noontide wakes anew
The buttercups, the little children's dower
- Far brighter than this gaudy melon-flower!

Robert Browning (1812 – 1889)

5   Jenny Sweeney
Appliqué with free machine embroidery and quilting

Arrival 1946

The boat docked in at Liverpool.
From the train Tariq stared
at the unbroken line of washing
from the north west to Euston.

These are strange people, he thought -
an Empire, and all this washing,
the underwear, the Englishman's garden.
It was Monday, and very sharp.

Moniza Alvi (1954 -   )

6   Wendy Ward
Fabric collage with machine stitching

Seascapes

Once I favoured cosy coasts,
Toytown harbours,
Bathtub boats,
Cottages in Dulux dream shades,
Thrusting pepper pot lighthouses.
Propinquity draws me to mud flats,
Trees clawing the shore line,
Garlanded with flotsam and jetsam,
Revealing root rubric,
Giving witness to lost land.
Rough shores like dumped building gravel
Bear reminders of human frailty,
Scattered with each tidal sweep.
Seabirds wailing and weeping
Cluster in myriad formations
Like children changing allegiance
In the playground.
They go in to draw
Safe Lilliputian landscapes
with tiny tugs and dancing dolphins.

Sue Flawn (1945 -   )

7   Yvonne Blatchford
Machine pieced and quilted

8   **Elizabeth Saunders**
    Hand embroidery on machine pieced fabric

A Picturesque Dream in Goathland

Smoothly flowing water trickles over jagged imperfect cobbled stone,
Hidden beneath the unruly undergrowth never to be known.

Can this secret garden be real?
The sensations too thrilling to be true,
Can this idealistic dream be what hopes are built from
Or was this peaceful imagery created to enslave me and you?

Then the deceitful treacherous pebbles show their hidden secret,
But... it's too late water flies and soars, falling to the waiting rocks.
It strikes with a cruel infliction enforcing all its strength,
Torment and misery will soon be shown through the stones hurt indent.

It glides away to pastures new sure to grow and mount and swell,
With the rains silent fall or the grasses dew no time to linger and dwell.
It flows swiftly on unknowing of what's to come,
Over craggy stones and animals' bones to the light sound of the dragonflies' hum.

Where will it go? What will it see?
The knowledge of this is not for you, or me!
But I'm sure we'll find in years from now the memory of this stream,
And the fresh scent of imagination is still... anything but a dream.

Louisa Saunders (1985 -   )

There's a Poem Hiding in Wan's Fish and Chip Shop

I'm certain there's a poem
Hiding somewhere in
Wan's Fish and Chip Shop.
I'm just not sure where.
I think of it whenever I climb the steps
To be greeted by those polite
And inscrutable smiles.
I'm sure it must be here, somewhere.
Perhaps it's in the giant basket
Of limpid lifeless chips,
Awaiting their searing fate.
Or among the cod fish bodies
Lovingly dressed in their floury coats.
Perhaps a fritter could be hiding the words,
Pineapple or pea. But more likely a saveloy.
Or a new fangled battered Mars Bar.
That would be a beauteous thing,
With its chin dribbling caramel
Inner secret. That would be too clever.
How about that clock though, that could be
The solution? Its grinning fish clock face
With wrought iron fingers, talking of the
One That got Away. That's poetry of a kind,
Maybe. Or this notice board in the corner

Where all and sundry advertise their wares and
Trades in language to entice, discover your
Fortune and lag your pipes in one easy
Location. Now this row of visually enticing
Sauces, they could be just the thing but
Which sachet conceals the stanzas,
That's difficult to fathom when there's
Ketchup, brown and curry.
But wait. What's this in pride of place,
Bold and brazen on the counter top.
The giant glassy eyed jar of pickled eggs,
I am sure we need look no further?
But the order is ready, I must depart,
Certain of the answer.
But no, now I spot the plastic condiments.
Shaken with flair and ease,
Tantalising each morsel with their
Vinegary tang.
There is a poem hiding in Wan's Fish and Chip
Shop.
But I'm just not sure where.

Pauline Hand (1953 -   )

9   Margaret Lappin
Free machine embroidery

10 **Bernadette Murphy**
Hand stitching

The Lake Isle of Innisfree

I will arise and go now, and go to Innisfree,
And a small cabin build there, of clay and wattles made:
Nine bean-rows will I have there, a hive for the honey-bee,
And live alone in the bee-loud glade.

And I shall have some peace there, for peace comes dropping slow,
Dropping from the veils of the morning to where the cricket sings;
There midnight's all a glimmer, and noon a purple glow,
And evening full of the linnet's wings.

I will arise and go now, for always night and day
I hear lake water lapping with low sounds by the shore;
While I stand on the roadway, or on the pavements grey,
I hear it in the deep heart's core.

W.B. Yeats (1865 – 1939)

'A Sense of Place' - Artists' Statements:

1 For Sale by W.H. Davies **Artist ISCA Tatters**: "The group liked the poem and thought we could use various tatting techniques to represent it."

2 Abbey Ruins by Margaret Crosfield **Artist Margaret Crosfield**: "Inspiration came from abbeys of which there are several in the area in which I live."

3 A New Home for Saxons by Alma Lusby **Artist Alma Harding**: "As it is almost 50 years since the poem was written and I was not allowed to do needlework at school, this seems a good time to portray the poem as I'd have wanted."

4 River Deben by Richard Stewart **Artist Anne-Marie Stewart**: "Sutton Hoo is just a few miles from our home and this poem is a reminder of the king, his ship burial and the importance of the nearby river."

5 Home Thoughts, from Abroad by Robert Browning **Artist Jenny Sweeney**: "I had to learn this poem in junior school. I loved it then and still do. It brings back strong memories of my childhood living close to the countryside and of the elms that surrounded us."

6 Arrival 1946 by Moniza Alvi **Artist Wendy Ward**: "The poem instantly conjured up images of jumbled textiles for me. I work a lot with recycled textiles which I use a lot in the picture. Immigration is a subject which is still current and the collaged textiles represent the patchwork of people that make up the population of the UK."

7 Seascapes by Sue Flawn **Artist Yvonne Blatchford**: "I have had this harbour fabric for ages and love it. The poem seemed the ideal way to use it and the dolphin fabric is the last piece of a design I have used before in lots of projects. I think they come together well and really illustrate the poem."

8 A Picturesque Dream in Goathland by Louisa Saunders **Artist Elizabeth Saunders**: "This poem was written by my daughter following a visit to the famous 'Heartbeat' village of Goathland in Yorkshire where we discovered a magical place of waterfall and undergrowth."

9 There's a poem hiding in Wan's Fish and Chip Shop by Pauline Hand **Artist Margaret Lappin:** "This poem is about a very ordinary subject. Most people will have spent time in the queue at the chip shop, dreaming away the time until it is their turn to be served."

10 The Lake Isle of Innisfree by W.B. Yeats **Artist Bernadette Murphy**: "The colours and romantic content of this poem gave me the inspiration and opportunity to create my own vision of the Lake Isle."

11 Rita Taylor
Hand embroidery

An Otter (extract)

Underwater eyes, an eel's
Oil of water body, neither fish nor beast is
        the otter:
Four-legged yet water-gifted, to outfish fish;
With webbed feet and long ruddering tail
And a round head like an old tomcat.

Brings the legend of himself
From before wars or burial, in spite of
        hounds and vermin-poles;
Does not take root like the badger.
        Wanders, cries;
Gallops along land he no longer belongs to;
Re-enters the water by melting.

Of neither water nor land. Seeking
Some world lost when first he dived, that he
        cannot come since,
Takes his changed body into the holes of lakes;
As if blind, cleaves the stream's push till he
        licks
The pebbles of the source; from sea

To sea crosses in three nights
Like a king in hiding. Crying to the old shape
        of the star land,
Over sunken farms where the bats go round,
Without answer. Till light and birdsong come
Walloping up roads with the milk wagon.

Ted Hughes (1930 – 1998)

The Touch of Nature

"Drifting meadow of the air,
Where bloom the daisied banks and violets..."

Henry David Thoreau

In this section we find descriptions of delicate, wind-tossed
blossoms side by side with portrayals of sharp-eyed hunters.
The predators of sky and stream swoop through the pages,
tempered by the soft whispers of mellow or enigmatic
natural beauty.

Blazing in gold and quenching in purple

Blazing in gold and quenching in purple
Leaping like leopards to the sky
Then at the feet of the old horizon
Laying her spotted face to die;
Stooping as low as the otter's window,
Touching the roof and tinting the barn,
Kissing her bonnet to the meadow -
And the Juggler of Day is gone!

Emily Dickinson (1830 – 1886)

12 Elaine Greatrex
Machine embroidery with appliqué, photo printing and fabric painting

Mist

Low-anchored cloud,
Newfoundland air,
Fountain head and source of rivers,
Dew-cloth, dream drapery,
And napkin spread by fays;
Drifting meadow of the air,
Where bloom the daisied banks and violets,
And in whose fenny labyrinth
The bittern booms and heron wades;
Spirit of the lake and seas and rivers,
Bear only perfumes and the scent
Of healing herbs to just men's fields!

Henry David Thoreau (1817 – 1862)

13 Janet Cairney
Raw edge appliqué with hand quilting

Daffodils

I wandered lonely as a cloud
That floats on high o'er vales and hills,
When all at once I saw a crowd,
A host, of golden daffodils;
Beside the lake, beneath the trees,
Fluttering and dancing in the breeze.

Continuous as the stars that shine
And twinkle on the milky way,
They stretched in never-ending line
Along the margin of a bay:
Ten thousand saw I at a glance,
Tossing their heads in sprightly dance.

The waves beside them danced, but they
Out-did the sparkling waves in glee;
A poet could not be but gay,
In such a jocund company!
I gazed- and gazed- but little thought
What wealth the show to me had brought:

For oft, when on my couch I lie
In vacant or in pensive mood,
They flash upon that inward eye
Which is the bliss of solitude;
And then my heart with pleasure fills,
And dances with the daffodils.

William Wordsworth (1770 – 1850)

14 Essex Shuttles
Fabric collage with tatting

15 Yvonne Blatchford
Machine pieced and quilted

The Lily

The modest Rose puts forth a thorn,
The humble sheep a threat'ning horn:
While the Lily white shall in love delight,
Nor a thorn nor a threat stain her beauty
bright.

William Blake (1757 – 1827)

16 Barbara Janssen
Image transfer, appliqué, fabric painting, machine quilting

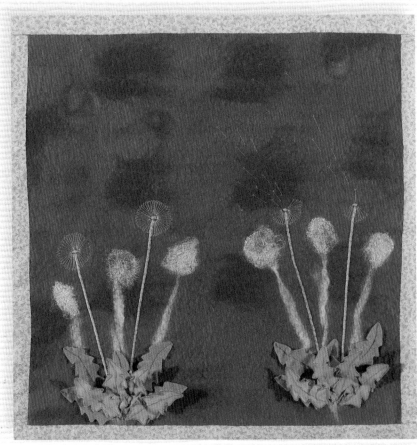

The Dandelion -
Nature's Sundial

17 Elizabeth Peters
Machine and hand stitching on felted fabric

18 Ann Smith
Chiffon strips with free machined flowers and seed heads on dissolvable fabric, embellished with beads, wire, wool taps and hand embroidery

The Dandelion - Nature's Sundial

My leaves are green and lushly spread,
My stem stands tall with a 'gilded' head,
My petals fan in yellow gold;
But I am a weed, or so I'm told.

Towards the sun, I gaze and smile:
Some say that I am Nature's dial;
But if I have such natural powers,
I only count the sunny hours!

More do I mark, when I turn grey,
A sphere of seeds in soft array,
Each tiny parachute a seed,
Born by the wind as another weed!

Christopher Daniel (1933 -   )

The Owl

When cats run home and light is come,
And dew is cold upon the ground,
And the far-off stream is dumb,
And the whirring sail goes round,
And the whirring sail goes round;
Alone and warming his five wits,
The white owl in the belfry sits.

When merry milkmaids click the latch,
And rarely smells the new-mown hay,
And the cock hath sung beneath the thatch
Twice or thrice his roundelay,
Twice or thrice his roundelay;
Alone and warming his five wits,
The white owl in the belfry sits.

Alfred, Lord Tennyson (1809 – 1892)

19 Amanda Green
Machine pieced with appliqué and hand embroidery

Dragonfly

Now let's have another try
To love the giant Dragonfly

Stand beside the peaceful water.
Next thing – a whispy, dry clatter

And he whizzes to a dead stop
In mid-air, and his eyes pop.

Snakey stripes, a snakey fright!
Does he sting? Does he bite?

Suddenly he's gone. Suddenly back. A
Scarey jumping cracker –

Here! Right here!
An inch from your ear!

Sizzling in the air
And giving you a stare

Out of the huge cockpit of his eye -!

Now say: 'What a lovely surprise!'

Ted Hughes (1930 – 1998)

20 Jo Baker
Machine and hand embroidery, applied embroidered net on painted silk

The Snail

At sunset, when the night-dew fall,
Out of the ivy on the wall
With horns outstretched and pointed tail
Comes the grey and noiseless snail.
On ivy stems she clambers down,
Carrying her house of brown.
Safe in the dark, no greedy eye
Can her tender body spy,
While she herself, a hungry thief,
Searches out the freshest leaf.
She travels on as best she can
Like a toppling caravan.

James Reeves (1909 – 1978)

21 Sheila Warman
Patchwork, appliqué, stumpwork, hand embroidery, machine quilted

22 Jenny Jarvis
Manipulated calico fabric with machine quilting, appliqué and hand embellishment

A Day by the Sea

The day's too dull for pocket cameras,
Their quick impressions of the changing scene,
And I've no skill with crayons or with paints
To catch the colours of the grey-green sea,
But what a picture's painted in my head,
Of surf-tossed kelpies racing for the shore
Risking their necks each time they reach the rocks
Recovering to race on as before
Only to break their backs upon the cliffs.

The off-white seagulls skirt across the sky
Drift with the wind and follow on the tide;
Intent on fishing now they seem to cry:
Come back, come back, come back and see us play
The sea is here forever, not one day.

Elizabeth Bewick (1919 -   )

The Vanishing Zebra

Somehow, he has pulled off his trick,
Slipped back into his element,
As if a conjuror has drawn back the curtain on the empty cage
To find him refracted by a million mirrors
Or concealed by the enveloping smoke of distant tribesmen's fires.

Who searches for him in that darkness
Blacker, now, than the Serengeti night?
Nature does not scour the shadowy plain
Carrying the moon like an ivory candle in her anxious hand.

But somewhere a puzzled, troubled zookeeper
Counts and recounts his captive herd in their evening paddock.

Con Connell (1949 -   )

23 Kate Dowty
Machine pieced and quilted

A Windy Day

This wind brings all dead things to life,
Branches that lash the air like whips
And dead leaves rolling in a hurry
On peering in a rabbit's bury
Or trying to push down a tree;
Gates that fly open to the wind
And close again behind
And make the cattle look like ships;
Straws glistening and stiff
Lying on air as on a shelf
And pond that leaps to leave itself;
And feathers too that rise and float,
Each feather changed into a bird,
And line-hung sheets that crack and strain;
Even the sun-greened coat,
That through so many winds has served,
The scarecrow struggles to put on again.

Andrew Young (1885 – 1971)

24 Isabel Hewitt
Appliqué with machine quilting

Today's Tomorrow

Today the seed -
Tomorrow the grain
Today the planting -
Tomorrow the gain.

Today's now -
Tomorrow's then.
Today's children -
Tomorrow's men.

Tonight's darkness -
Tomorrow's light.
Tonight's blindness -
Tomorrow's sight.

Today's swords -
Tomorrow's ploughs.
Today's decisions -
Tomorrow's now.

Pat Moon (1946 -   )

25 Jolene Smith
Machine stitched plastics and fabric with seed and bead embellishment

'The Touch of Nature' - Artists' Statements:

11 An Otter by Ted Hughes   **Artist Rita Taylor**:   "I particularly enjoy depicting animals. The description of the otter with its tomcat head appealed, as did the imagery of the underwater world."

12 Blazing in Gold by Emily Dickinson   **Artist Elaine Greatrex**:   "I have recently spent a lot of time at my mother's house in Spain. This is the view from her patio of the sun going down over the Mongo Mountains (the Sleeping Indian)."

13 Mist by Henry Thoreau   **Artist Janet Cairney**:   "I enjoyed all the poems in the Poetry in Stitches booklet but because I like to make abstract works with a reference to landscapes, this poem appealed particularly."

14 Daffodils by William Wordsworth   **Artists Essex Shuttles** (E.Law, P.Brooks, C.Dawson, M.Horley, P.Hagan, J.Powell, R.Perkins, K.Wilson, D.Badger, D.Clark):   "We all felt inspired by this poem and felt we could interpret it well."

15 Daffodils by William Wordsworth   **Artist Yvonne Blatchford**:   "I have always liked Wordsworth's poem about daffodils and they are my husband's favourite flower, hence these are 'Daffodils for Brian.'"

16 The Lily by William Blake   **Artist Barbara Janssen**:   "This poem stimulated the strongest visual image in my head. I love lilies and always have a spray in my kitchen. I loved the contrast between the sharp thorn of the beautiful rose and the lily which has nothing but beauty to offer the beholder – unless, of course, one is allergic to the pollen!"

17 The Dandelion by Christopher Daniel   **Artist Elizabeth Peters**:   "I chose this poem as it sort of reminded me of me. I love raised embroidery and wanted the piece to stand out. I used felt as it is a natural fibre and the poem is about nature."

18 The Dandelion by Christopher Daniel   **Artist Ann Smith**:   "The dandelion is altogether bright, edible to some creatures and very efficient at spreading itself around – even without the help of children!"

19 The Owl by Alfred, Lord Tennyson   **Artist Amanda Green**:   "Owls are rarely seen in the wild, so to see the world from the owl's perspective seemed unusual and challenging. Also, Tennyson is my favourite poet."

20 Dragonfly by Ted Hughes   **Artist Jo Baker**:   "I could empathise with the sentiments in this poem."

21 The Snail by James Reeves   **Artist Sheila Warman**:   "I wanted a poem with a strong visual identity, and a story that was easy to represent."

22 A Day by the Sea by Elizabeth Bewick   **Artist Jenny Jarvis**:   "This is my interpretation of a very special place in Norfolk, Snettisham Beach, a beautiful place where we visit for just one day but return often. The shells for this piece were collected whilst paddling and walking from Snettisham to Heacham."

23 The Vanishing Zebra by Con Connell   **Artist Kate Dowty**:   "Over the years I have accumulated, but rarely used, a variety of black and white printed fabrics including one with zebra stripes. This was the perfect opportunity to use some of them and a log cabin technique seemed to achieve the right effect."

24 A Windy Day by Andrew Young   **Artist Isabel Hewitt**:   "I was inspired by the pictures done by Gordon Beningfield in his books."

25 Today's Tomorrow by Pat Moon   **Artist Jolene Smith**:   "The amount of rubbish which goes into the landfill upsets me. I believe that we should recycle as 'tomorrow is now'."

26 Linda Connell
Hand and machine quilting on cotton fabrics with bead embellishment

Love in a Cold Climate

I was scraping the ice off the windscreen
And it made me remember, way back
When me and the missus were courting
And we lived in that freezing cold flat.

We'd get up so late at the weekends -
The bed was the snug place to stay -
That we'd only just make it for kick off
(And we'd have to run most of the way!)

Then one wintry day in the New Year
With ice on the window, so thick
That we'd sprint to the kitchen or bathroom,
And then we'd dash back, pretty quick!

And I thought of the bed, and the stadium,
And I turned to the missus and said,
"We don't have to go to the football,
We can do something different instead......"

She sat up in bed, looking outraged,
And threw back the sheets with both hands,
"Do you think I'd miss one minute's football?
Leave that to the fair-weather fans!"

"So what if it's two below zero?
Who cares if it's threatening to sleet?
At quarter to three, you know where I'll be
And that's warming my favourite seat!"

Now I'm scraping the ice off the windscreen
While her and the kids, in the car,
Are chanting their favourite anthem
In praise of the team's latest star.

And the warmth that we shared hasn't left us -
But doubled - from two seats to four.
And if warmth was a chant, we'd be deafening.
And if warmth was a goal, then we'd score.

Con Connell (1949 -   )

Words of Love

"Tenderly, gently, I unlock your heart..."

Con Connell

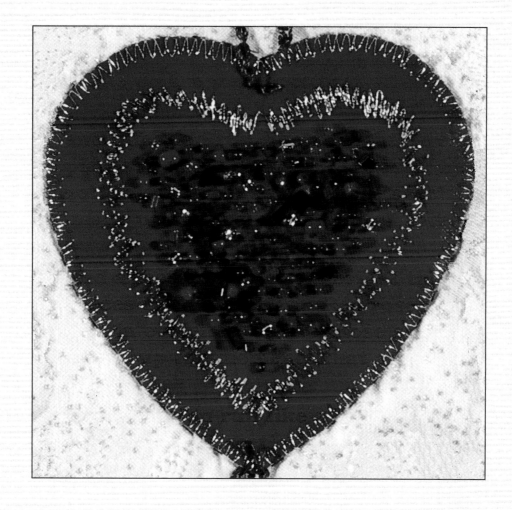

Tenderness and affection run like a bright thread through each of the pieces in this section. Red roses, hearts, and valentines are all in evidence, as are those special words and images that make up the moments that all lovers cherish.

i carry your heart with me
(i carry it in

i carry your heart with me(i carry it in
my heart)i am never without it(anywhere
i go you go,my dear;and whatever is done
by only me is your doing,my darling)
                       i fear
no fate(for you are my fate,my sweet)i want
no world(for beautiful you are my world,my true)
and it's you are whatever a moon has always meant
and whatever a sun will always sing is you

here is the deepest secret nobody knows
(here is the root of the root and the bud of the bud
and the sky of the sky of a tree called life;which grows
higher than the soul can hope or mind can hide)
and this is the wonder that's keeping the stars apart

i carry your heart(i carry it in my heart)

E.E. Cummings (1894 – 1962)

27 Dos Amigas
*Appliqué with machine embroidery and hand
sewn embellishments*

28 Helen McNicoll
Rug Hooking

Love

Love bade me welcome; yet my soul drew back,
  Guilty of dust and sin.
But quick-eyed Love, observing me grow slack
  From my first entrance in,
Drew nearer to me, sweetly questioning
  If I lack'd anything.

'A guest,' I answer'd, 'worthy to be here:'
  Love said, 'You shall be he.'
'I, the unkind, ungrateful? Ah, my dear,
  I cannot look on Thee.'
Love took my hand and smiling did reply,
  'Who made the eyes but I?'

'Truth, Lord; but I have marr'd them: let my shame
  Go where it doth deserve.'
'And know you not,' says Love, 'Who bore the blame?'
  'My dear, then I will serve.'
'You must sit down,' says Love, 'and taste my meat.'
  So I did sit and eat.

George Herbert (1593 -1633)

29 Jayne Lewis
Image transfer with free machine embroidery, quilting, fabric paint and beading

Tea

I like pouring your tea, lifting
the heavy pot, and tipping it up,
so the fragrant liquid streams in your china cup.

Or when you're away, or at work,
I like to think of your cupped hands as you sip,
as you sip, of the faint half-smile of your lips.

I like the questions - sugar? - milk? -
and the answers I don't know by heart, yet,
for I see your soul in your eyes, and I forget.

Jasmine, Gunpowder, Assam, Earl Grey, Ceylon,
I love tea's names. Which tea would you like? I say
but it's any tea for you, please, any time of day,

as the women harvest the slopes
for the sweetest leaves, on Mount Wu-Yi,
and I am your lover, smitten, straining your tea.

Carol Ann Duffy (1955 -   )

Valentine

Not a red rose or a satin heart.

I give you an onion.
It is a moon wrapped in brown paper.
It promises light
like the careful undressing of love.

Here.
It will blind you with tears
like a lover.
It will make your reflection
a wobbling photo of grief.

I am trying to be truthful.

Not a cute card or kissogram.

I give you an onion.
Its fierce kiss will stay on your lips,
possessive and faithful
as we are,
for as long as we are.

Take it.
Its platinum loops shrink to a wedding ring,
if you like.
Lethal.
Its scent will cling to your fingers,
cling to your knife.

Carol Ann Duffy (1955 -   )

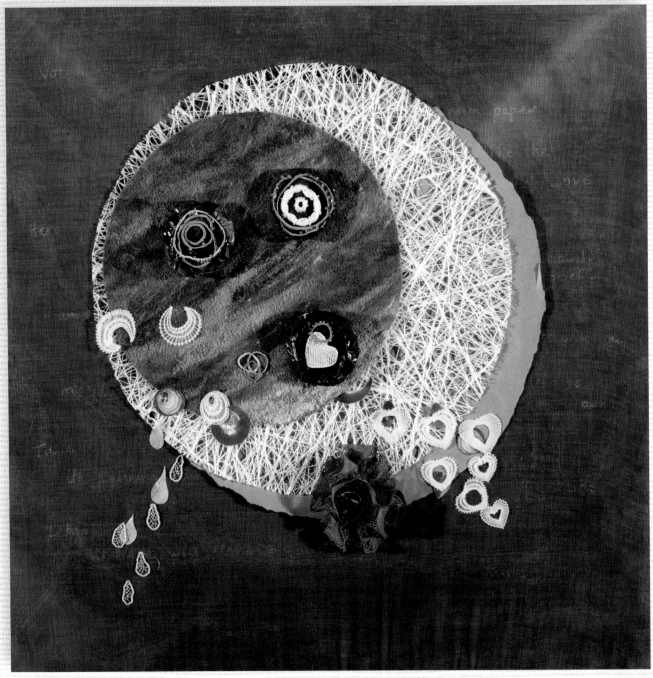

30 Atelier 90
Bobbin and needle lace on paper and dyed fabric

31 June Hurst
Beads on cotton fabric, machine stitching

Jewels of Love

I know of a beauty, a beryl most bright,
As lovely to look on as silver-foiled sapphire,
As gentle as jasper - a gleam in the light,
As true as the ruby, or garnet in gold
Like onyx she is esteemed in the height;
A diamond of worth when she's dressed for the day;
Like coral her lustre, like Caesar or knight;
Like emerald at morning, this maiden has might.
My precious red stone, with the power of a pearl,
I pick for her prettiness, excellent girl!

Anon. Medieval.

A Red, Red Rose

My love is like a red, red rose,
That's newly sprung in June.
My love is like the melody,
That's sweetly played in tune.

As fair art thou, my bonnie lass,
So deep in love am I,
And I will love thee still, my Dear,
Till all the seas gang dry.

Till all the seas gang dry, my Dear,
And the rocks melt with the sun!
And I will love thee still, my Dear,
While the sands of life shall run.

And fare thee well, my only Love,
And fare thee well a while!
And I will come again, my Love,
'Though it were ten thousand mile!

Robert Burns (1759 – 1796)

32 Isabell Bourke
Hand and machine embroidery

33 Karin Schaffer-Keddy
Appliqué, hand and machine embroidery

The Cello Player
(Bach Suite No 6 in D major – prélude)

I would crawl across a warm, bare floor
In a long, black dress
To watch you caress her polished brown
curves
While you stroke her throat
Stretched taut and ready to be ensnared
By the breath of the finest stallion's tail
Blown over her four prison bars of spun metal
and sinew

I would have you spark the fire of pure music
and watch you spill a song from her heart
Like a velvet scream
And with deep and resonant beckoning
She sighs an alarming outpouring of frantic
welcome

I would sit so still and mesmerised
And want for nothing

And would need nothing
Until the last, long note…
Then I would need you too…

I would be your cello - you would hold me so
And caress my polished brown curves
And stroke my throat and kiss my neck
And let the long, black dress fall to the warm,
bare floor
I would be stretched taut until your own
breath would spark my fire
And I would sigh an alarming outpouring of
frantic welcome

I would be mesmerised
While your hands played over me until
My long, last note…

Harriet Green (1953 -   )

34 Yvonne Blatchford and Linda Connell
Cotton fabrics machine pieced and quilted

35 Sue Gransby
Fabric collage with machine stitching

The sun has burst the sky

The sun has burst the sky
Because I love you
And the river its banks.

The sea laps the great rocks
Because I love you
And takes no heed of the moon dragging it away
And saying coldly 'Constancy is not for you'.
The blackbird fills the air
Because I love you
With spring and lawns and shadows falling on lawns.

The people walk in the street and laugh
I love you
And far down the river ships sound their hooters
Crazy with joy because I love you.

Jenny Joseph (1932 -   ) © Jenny Joseph

36 Judith Hanley
Hand stitching on plastic and canvas

Enigma

Looking for clues to decipher your love -
A sigh, or a sideways look
Might reveal how you feel when your warm lips touch mine
As I decode your life like a book.

Watching your face as you sleep by my side
Years of life etched in your skin,
Stretched like a code that attempts to conceal
The message that's hidden within.

Counting the times that I've whispered your name
Making the numbers make sense.
Searching for patterns that seem to be there,
Wary of any pretence.

Tenderly, gently, I unlock your heart -
Easing my mind through its doors -
And lay bare, before you, the love that I have.
'And all that I have will be yours.'

Con Connell (1949 -   )

The theme of this poem draws upon 'The Life that I have' by Leo Marks.

'Words of Love' - Artists' Statements:

26 Love in a Cold Climate by Con Connell **Artist Linda Connell**: "Con is Poet in Residence at Southampton Football Club, and with three sons supporting Southampton and Arsenal, both red and white, I wanted to choose a football poem. This one is funny but reflects the closeness of family."

27 i carry your heart with me(i carry it in by E.E. Cummings **Artists Dos Amigas** (Janice Cornwall & Pauline McMillan): "We were both visually inspired by the depth of emotion this poem conveys. In the simplest of words the author envelopes our own hearts and minds. We also love the heart shape."

28 Love by George Herbert **Artist Helen McNicoll**: "This poem has inspired me on my spiritual journey. The utter love of God and the desire to share love is so simply expressed and I wanted to try and capture some of that uncompromising 'open door' love, in rug hooking."

29 Tea by Carol Ann Duffy **Artist Jayne Lewis**: "As soon as I read the poem I thought of the many kinds of tea and all the different packaging. I also thought of the wonderful pretty tea sets that were around when I was a child."

30 Valentine by Carol Ann Duffy **Artists Atelier 90** (Ann Forbes Cockell, Angela Jennings, Julie Nichols, Jean Rooke, Ruth Walker, Jill Woodhouse): "Whilst studying the works of Carol Ann Duffy, one of our group recognised the potential for the visual interpretation of the poem 'Valentine' into a textile image."

31 Jewels of Love by Anon. **Artist June Hurst**: "As my last piece of Poetry in Stitches work 'The Green Man' was medieval, I liked the idea of using the same idea and historical time."

32 A Red, Red Rose by Robert Burns **Artist Isabell Bourke**: "I like the poem and also the song of the same name. It is romantic and expressive of feeling by the author."

33 The Cello Player by Harriet Green **Artist Karin Schaffer-Keddy**: "This poem is both sensuous and sensual."

34 The Sun has Burst the Sky by Jenny Joseph **Artists Yvonne Blatchford and Linda Connell**: "We both like Jenny Joseph's poems and this poem lent itself to a traditional stained glass technique inspired by the roof windows of the Metropolitan Cathedral of Christ the King in Liverpool and a talk by Gail Lawther."

35 The Sun has Burst the Sky by Jenny Joseph **Artist Sue Gransby**: "I chose this poem because of its first line. In my mind I immediately saw a huge exploding sun and wanted to create a bright and joyous piece of work to match the mood of the poem."

36 Enigma by Con Connell **Artist Judith Hanley**: "Poetry like codes has a hidden meaning. I have tried to show the links between them in this hand embroidery. There are seven different stitches covering two types of canvas, plastic and canvas. The different colours show a letter and a morse code which decode into words and a phrase from the poem."

37 Mary Langley
Free Machine Embroidery

Tree Prayer

You who would pass by
And raise your hand against me
- Listen before you harm me.
I am the heat in your hearth
On long winter nights;
The friendly shade screening you from the
summer sun,
And my fruits are refreshing draughts.

I am the beam that holds your house
The board of your table
The bed on which you lie
And the timber which builds your boat.

I am the handle of your hoe,
And the door of your homestead,

I am the wood of your cradle,
And the shell of your coffin.

I am the gift of God and friend of man.
You who pass by me
Listen to my prayer
And harm me not.

Anon.

Spiritual Reflections

"My soul, there is a country
Far beyond the stars..."

Henry Vaughan

Poetry has the power to reach deep into the soul, stirring strong, even passionate, feelings. In this section, we find philosophical and contemplative poems expressing some of the ideas which influence the way our poets and artists experience their spiritual environment.

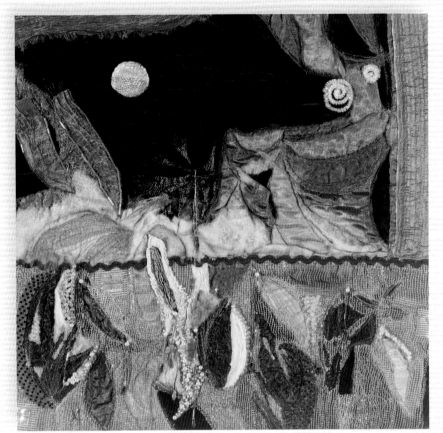

Windmills of the Night

Veils of cloth, veils of gold
Beating, beating breath
Dreaming, sleeping depths of night
The fleeting lights of home

Drifting, drifting clouds of flight
Searching, searching piercing light
Whirling wheels to embrace
Lying in a lake of grace

Veils of cloth, veils of gold
Windmills of the night behold!

Webs of life, webs of soul
Drifting, drifting breath
Swirling in the sparks of stars
The velvet hues of night

Whispering winds, caressing storms
Creating everlasting thoughts
Breathing through the midnight bloom
The colours of a distant moon

Veils of cloth, veils of gold
Windmills of the night behold!

Dawn Ashcroft (1947 -   )

38 Dawn Ashcroft
Layered fabrics with bead embellishment. Hand and machine embroidery

Doing the Big Bang Theory

In holes in holes in holes in gaps
in holes in holes

the light darkens shadows
of the ghost that loves the most,
and you are huge but I am getting bigger,

filling our brilliant emptiness
with the inevitable gravity flow
of our indecipherable rivers,

is it you that knows the knows that knows
or me?
because the soon is becoming nower.

And it will be this act of us blowing our
                              bobble-hats off
That creates a truth,
or is this friction, fiction?

As you climb my tree to touch the hem
of my painful extremities,
please, please, please, never come down again.

Matt Nunn (1971 -   )

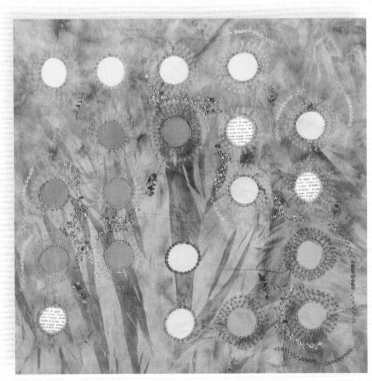

39 Theresa Nunn
Dyed fabric, reverse appliqué, machine and hand stitching

The Loom of Time

Man's life is laid in the loom of time
To a pattern he does not see,
While the weavers work and the shuttles fly
Till the dawn of eternity.

Some shuttles are filled with silver threads
And some with threads of gold,
While often but the darker hues
Are all that they may hold.

But the weaver watches with skilful eye
Each shuttle fly to and fro,
And sees the pattern so deftly wrought
As the loom moves sure and slow.

God surely planned the pattern:
Each thread, the dark and fair,
Is chosen by His master skill
And placed in the web with care.

He only knows its beauty,
And guides the shuttles which hold
The threads so unattractive,
As well as the threads of gold.

Not till each loom is silent,
And the shuttles cease to fly,
Shall God reveal the pattern
And explain the reason why

The dark threads were as needful
In the weaver's skilful hand
As the threads of gold and silver
For the pattern which He planned.

Anon.

40 Christine Pulker
Machine embroidery with layered silk chiffon, voile, net and ribbons

On Change of Weathers

And were it for thy profit to obtain
All sunshine? No vicissitude of rain?
Thinkest thou that thy laborious plough requires
Not winter frosts, as well as summer fires?
There must be both: sometimes these hearts of ours
Must have the sweet, the seasonable showers
Of tears; sometimes, the frost of chill despair
Makes our desirèd sunshine seem more fair:
Weathers that most oppose to flesh and blood,
Are such as help to make our harvest good:
We may not choose, great God; it is thy task:
We know not what to have, nor how to ask.

Francis Quarles (1592 -1644)

41 Mary Dorgan
Patchwork with hand and machine stitching

42 Jenny Longhurst
Machine piecing and appliqué

Ah! Sunflower

Ah! Sunflower, weary of time,
Who countest the steps of the sun;
Seeking after that sweet golden clime
Where the traveller's journey is done;

Where the Youth pined away with desire,
And the pale virgin shrouded in snow,
Arise from their graves, and aspire
Where my Sunflower wishes to go!

William Blake (1757 – 1827)

The Story of Creation

When God created Heaven and Earth, so the Bible says
He started on a Monday and it took him seven days,
Well six really – perhaps he was a woman.....
Gazing at the wastelands of water dark and deep
He decided what was needed first and light began to creep,
In order to appreciate the light, one must first experience the dark......
On Tuesday God decided to create the Heavens above
He divided up the water with one almighty shove
As above, so below......
Wednesday was to see more parting of the water,
Seas were formed and land appeared in each and every quarter,
And on the land grew herbs and trees, a covering of grass,
Trees with fruit and plants with seeds soon appeared en masse,
And God liked what he saw, and thought he would do more....tomorrow

Thursday soon proved to be a very busy day,
The sun, the moon, the stars were formed along the milky way,
The days and years were all marked out –the seasons would be four,
And the signs up in the heavens would be there for evermore,
Shining on the earth below, the sun was hot and bright,
When darkness fell the moon appeared to lighten up the night
Twinkle, twinkle, little star, up above the world so far......
Thursday passed to Friday, producing wildlife by the score,
The waters teemed with fish, and creatures swam offshore,
Looking to the skies above, for he had more plans in mind,
Soon our feathered friends appeared, of each and every kind,
All things bright and beautiful, all creatures great and small....

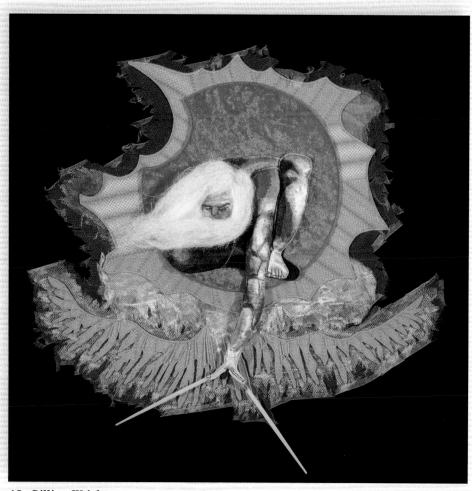

43 Gillian Wright
Stumpwork with machine stitching

On Saturday God turned once more to the land beyond the seas,
More living creatures then appeared, and animals climbed the trees,
And God liked what he saw, but he knew he could do more.
So God created Adam to walk upon the land,
And very soon Eve followed, to take him by the hand,
Everything has its opposite and it's equal....
Sunday dawned and God was pleased with everything he saw
He decided that his work was done and he would do no more,
What's needed now is a day of rest, no need to work he said
To recover from the week before and prepare for the one ahead,
So the seventh day was blessed, and the Sabbath day made holy
When on the breeze he heard a cry 'a day of rest? Oh yeah, if only!'
A woman's work is never done.....or was it?

Gillian Wright (1949 -   )

44 Linda Mottram
Hand and machine embroidery with appliqué and bead embellishment

De Profundis

Oh why is earth set so remote?
I cannot reach the nearest star
That hangs afloat.

Oh why is heaven built so far,

I would not care to reach the moon,
One round monotonous of change;
Yet even she repeats her tune
Beyond my range.

I never watch the scatter'd fire
Of stars, or sun's far-trailing train,
But all my heart is one desire,
And all in vain:

For I am bound with fleshly bands,
Joy, beauty, lie beyond my scope;
I strain my heart, I stretch my hands,
And catch at hope.

Christina Rossetti   (1830 – 1894)

45 Victoria Ewing
Painted fabric with appliqué, machine, and hand stitching

46 Evelyn Bernardi
Hand embroidery and beading on painted and layered fabric

When Earth's past picture is painted

47 Mary Willars
Appliqué, machine and hand embroidery

When Earth's last picture is painted
And the tubes are twisted and dried,
When the oldest colours have faded,
And the youngest critic has died,
We shall rest, and faith, we shall need it -
Lie down for an aeon or two,
Till the Master of All Good Workmen
Shall put us to work anew.
And those that were good shall be happy:
They shall sit in a golden chair;
They shall splash at a ten league canvas
With brushes of comets' hair.
They shall find real saints to draw from -
Magdalene, Peter, and Paul;
They shall work for an age at a sitting
And never be tired at all!
And only the Master shall praise us,
And only the Master shall blame;
And no one shall work for the money,
And no one shall work for the fame,
But each for the joy of the working,
And each, in his separate star,
Shall draw the Thing as he sees It
For the God of Things as They are!

Rudyard Kipling (1865 – 1936)

Peace

MY soul, there is a country
    Far beyond the stars,
Where stands a winged sentry
    All skilful in the wars:
There, above noise and danger,
    Sweet Peace sits crown'd with smiles,
And One born in a manger
    Commands the beauteous files.
He is thy gracious Friend,
    And - O my soul, awake! -
Did in pure love descend
    To die here for thy sake.
If thou canst get but thither,
    There grows the flower of Peace,
The Rose that cannot wither,
    Thy fortress, and thy ease.
Leave then thy foolish ranges;
    For none can thee secure
But One who never changes -
    Thy God, thy life, thy cure.

Henry Vaughan (1621 – 1695)

48 Vivien Stamford
Hand stitched face on pieced fabric circle set on hessian

Psalm 23

The LORD is my shepherd; I have
everything I need.
He lets me rest in green meadows; he leads
me beside peaceful streams.
He renews my strength. He guides me along
right paths, bringing honour to his name.

Even when I walk through the dark valley of
death,
I will not be afraid, for you are close to me.
Your rod and your staff comfort and protect
me.

You prepare a feast for me in the presence
of my enemies: You welcome me as a guest,
anointing my head with oil.
My cup overflows with blessings.
Surely your goodness and unfailing love will
pursue me all the days of my life,
and I will live in the house of the LORD
forever.

Bible – *New Living Translation*

49 Delia Garrod
Canvas work with drawn thread work and appliqué

'Spiritual Reflections' - Artists' Statements:

37 Tree Prayer Anon. **Artist Mary Langley**: "I chose this poem because of my love for trees and the important role they play in climate control among other things."

38 Windmills of the Night by Dawn Ashcroft **Artist Dawn Ashcroft**: "I have written this poem as an imaginative expression of our night-time dream state. Creative design with mood, motion, and trance-like grace."

39 Doing the Big Band Theory by Matt Nunn **Artist Theresa Nunn**: "When reading this particular poem the images and colours in my mind instantaneously just 'happened' naturally; there was no tension involved. Beads provide the 'explosion'."

40 The Loom of Time Anon. **Artist Christine Pulker**: "The poem shows the progress of life from beginning of the life-force (the strands coming from the 'source' to the baby and mother), to the end (the hand of death gathering the life-force back); the circle of the pattern of that life having been pre-destined. Some good times - lighter hues, and some not such good times, darker hues. Only at the end is the purpose of the pattern revealed."

41 On Change of Weathers by Francis Quarles **Artist Mary Dorgan**: "I enjoyed the poem and instantly saw the work that I wanted to do. It is four patchwork strips of the seasons with hand and machine stitched plants, flowers etc."

42 Ah! Sunflower by William Blake **Artist Jenny Longhurst**: "The bright colours of sunflowers and their cheerful appearance has always appealed to me and I enjoyed the chance to illustrate William Blake's poem."

43 The Story of Creation by Gillian Wright **Artist Gillian Wright**: "I came across this painting 'The Ancient of Days or God creating the Universe' by William Blake. Although Blake wrote poetry, this was the frontispiece for his book 'Europe: A Prophecy'."

44 De Produndis by Christina Rossetti **Artist Linda Mottram**: "I like the abstract qualities of the poem and have translated the words into an abstract style picture which I hope conveys the true message of the poem – that you always strive to touch the beauty of the universe but can never quite reach it. The freestyle technique used conveys the sense of universe and the glittering beauty of the sea, the earth and the heavens."

45 De Produndis by Christina Rossetti **Artist Victoria Ewing**: "I was simply looking for a poem which embroidered a beautiful picture into my mind without me even thinking. De Profundis was immediately inspiring; I was captivated and found the sentiment elevating. After first painting the design I experimented with textures, colours, embroidery and a lot of Angelina fibre."

46 When Earth's last picture is painted by Rudyard Kipling **Artist Evelyn Bernardi**: "I found it a beautiful, sensitive poem and it reflects how I feel about being an artist."

47 When Earth's last picture is painted by Rudyard Kipling **Artist Mary Willars**: "I chose this poem because I enjoy painting and poetry and with the sewing everything I enjoy was encapsulated in one piece of work."

48 Peace by Henry Vaughan **Artist Vivien Stamford**: "In this embroidery I have tried to recapture the feeling of peace I experienced when visiting the Chora Church (museum) in Istanbul."

49 Psalm 23 Artist Delia Garrod: "Psalm 23 is a well known poem which people often appreciate in time of sadness or trouble. I hope seeing the shepherd helping and rescuing the sheep will show the way through the cross to find love, joy, peace, and new life on this earth and in the life to come."

50 Claire Benson
Fabric collage with machine and hand stitching

A Tent

A tent went up on the grass:
just room for a boy and his brother,
who waited for day to pass -
kept wishing that day would pass
as they'd never wished of another.
At last they got their wish.
Darkness fell and off they went
feeling quite daredevilish -
yes, really daredevilish -
to spend a night in that tent.

Night is dizzy and deep;
the wall of a tent is thin;
they were almost too scared to sleep,
but whispered each other to sleep
as stars and ghosts listened in.
And the tent flew through the night
on the back of the turning world,
which brought them home all right,
them and the tent, still upright
and now lavishly dew-pearled.

Christopher Reid (1949 -   )

Backward Glances

"And laughs the immortal river still,
Under the mill, under the mill?"

Rupert Brooke

Memories can sometimes be full of pleasure, sometimes pain. This section embraces a range of emotions, through remembrance of lost loved ones or ruined places, and the recollections of the happy times of childhood.

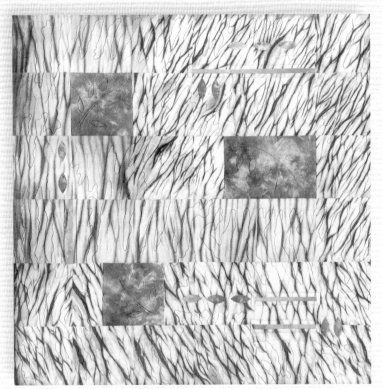

51 Anne-Marie Stewart
'Scrunch' and shibori dyeing, machine piecing, appliqué and quilting

In Memoriam –
Friday October 16ᵗʰ 1987

It is a morning for trees:

For suddenly seeing great holes
Punched and fixed in the garden sky
Where boughs had hung, long and pendulous
From the willow. Too big, we always said,
But now leaving an emptiness
That will never again be filled
In our lifetime. And the deep
Yellow glowing cascades of colour
Drain away as the laburnum reels
At a crazy angle. The great fir, too
Which tossed and swayed in every gale
Like the tall mast of a storm-set ship,
Has snapped at last. And we too
Flounder in the turmoil of another storm
Somewhere deep within, tugging at the memory
Of calmer days. We stand mute before
This awful majesty, numbed by disbelief:

It is a mourning for trees.

Richard Stewart (1945 -   )

Rock Me To Sleep (extract)

Backward, turn backward, O time, in your flight,
Make me a child again just for to-night!
Mother, come back from the echoless shore,
Take me again to your heart as of yore;
Kiss from my forehead the furrows of care,
Smooth the few silver threads out of my hair;
Over my slumbers your loving watch keep:
Rock me to sleep, Mother - rock me to sleep!

Backward, flow backward, oh, tide of the years!
I am so weary of toil and of tears
Toil without recompense, tears all in vain -
Take them, and give me my childhood again!
I have grown weary of dust and decay -
Weary of flinging my soul-wealth away;
Weary of sowing for others to reap;
Rock me to sleep, Mother - rock me to sleep!

Elizabeth Allen (1832 – 1911)

52 Hilary Sugai
Hand embroidery on hand dyed fabric

53 Hilary Burton
Machine pieced and hand quilted

54 Anne Reardon-James
Leather and cotton, hand stitched

Handbag

My mother's old leather handbag,
crowded with letters she carried
all through the war. The smell
of my mother's handbag: mints
and lipstick and Coty powder.
The look of those letters, softened
and worn at the edges, opened,
read, and refolded so often.
Letters from my father. Odour
of leather and powder, which ever
since then has meant womanliness,
and love, and anguish, and war.

Ruth Fainlight (1931 -)

"Is my team ploughing..."

'Is my team ploughing,
That I was used to drive
And hear the harness jingle
When I was man alive?'

Ay, the horses trample,
The harness jingles now;
No change though you lie under
The land you used to plough.

'Is football playing
Along the river shore,
With lads to chase the leather,
Now I stand up no more?'

Ay, the ball is flying,
The lads play heart and soul;
The goal stands up, the keeper
Stands up to keep the goal.

'Is my girl happy,
That I thought hard to leave,
And has she tired of weeping
As she lies down at eve?'

Ay, she lies down lightly,
She lies not down to weep:
Your girl is well contented.
Be still, my lad, and sleep.

'Is my friend hearty,
Now I am thin and pine,
And has he found to sleep in
A better bed than mine?'

Yes, lad, I lie easy,
I lie as lads would choose;
I cheer a dead man's sweetheart,
Never ask me whose.

A. E. Housman (1859 – 1936)

55 Veronica Hall
Locker-hooking on canvas, hand embroidery on felt, with cut chenille earth

56 **Elizabeth Brayshaw**
Machine appliqué and quilting

In Flanders Fields

In Flanders fields the poppies blow
Between the crosses, row on row,
That mark our place; and in the sky
The larks, still bravely singing, fly
Scarce heard amid the guns below.

We are the Dead. Short days ago
We lived, felt dawn, saw sunset glow,
Loved and were loved, and now we lie
In Flanders fields.

Take up our quarrel with the foe:
To you from failing hands we throw
The torch; be yours to hold it high.
If ye break faith with us who die
We shall not sleep, though poppies grow
In Flanders fields.

John McCrae *(1872 -1918)*

57 Jill Findlay
Appliqué with machine embroidery

The Little Dancers

Lonely, save for a few faint stars, the sky
dreams; and lonely, below, the little street
into its gloom retires, secluded and shy.
Scarcely the dumb roar enters this soft retreat;
and all is dark, save where come flooding rays
from a tavern-window; there, to the brisk measure
of an organ that down in an alley merrily plays,
two children, all alone and no one by,
holding their tattered frocks, thro' an airy maze
of motion lightly threaded with nimble feet
dance sedately; face to face they gaze,
their eyes shining, grave with a perfect pleasure.

Laurence Binyon (1869 – 1943)

My Last Duchess

That's my last Duchess painted on the wall,
Looking as if she were alive. I call
That piece a wonder, now: Frà Pandolf's hands
Worked busily a day, and there she stands.
Will't please you sit and look at her? I said
"Frà Pandolf" by design, for never read
Strangers like you that pictured countenance,
The depth and passion of its earnest glance,
But to myself they turned (since none puts by
The curtain I have drawn for you, but I)
And seemed as they would ask me, if they durst,
How such a glance came there; so, not the first
Are you to turn and ask thus. Sir, 'twas not
Her husband's presence only, called that spot
Of joy into the Duchess' cheek: perhaps
Frà Pandolf chanced to say "Her mantle laps
Over my lady's wrist too much," or "Paint
Must never hope to reproduce the faint
Half-flush that dies along her throat": such stuff
Was courtesy, she thought, and cause enough
For calling up that spot of joy. She had
A heart - how shall I say? - too soon made glad,
Too easily impressed; she liked whate'er
She looked on, and her looks went everywhere.
Sir, 'twas all one! My favour at her breast,
The dropping of the daylight in the West,
The bough of cherries some officious fool
Broke in the orchard for her, the white mule
She rode with round the
terrace all and each
Would draw from her alike
the approving speech,
Or blush, at least. She
thanked men - good! but
thanked
Somehow - I know not
how - as if she ranked
My gift of a nine-hundred-
years-old name
With anybody's gift. Who'd
stoop to blame
This sort of trifling? Even
had you skill

In speech (which I have not) to make your will
Quite clear to such a one, and say, "Just this
Or that in you disgusts me; here you miss,
Or there exceed the mark" - and if she let
Herself be lessoned so, nor plainly set
Her wits to yours, forsooth, and make excuse,
E'en then would be some stooping; and I choose
Never to stoop. Oh sir, she smiled, no doubt,
Whene'er I passed her; but who passed without
Much the same smile? This grew; I gave commands;
Then all smiles stopped together. There she stands
As if alive. Will't please you rise? We'll meet
The company below, then. I repeat,
The Count your master's known munificence
Is ample warrant that no just pretence
Of mine for dowry will be disallowed;
Though his fair daughter's self, as I avowed
At starting, is my object. Nay we'll go
Together down, sir. Notice Neptune, though,
Taming a sea-horse, thought a rarity,
Which Claus of Innsbruck cast in bronze for me!

Robert Browning (1812 – 1889)

58 Margaret Barraclough
Appliqué and hand embroidery with bead embellishment on felt

The Old Vicarage, Grantchester (extract)

Just now the lilac is in bloom,
All before my little room;
And in my flower-beds, I think,
Smile the carnation and the pink;
And down the borders, well I know,
The poppy and the pansy blow . . .
Oh! there the chestnuts, summer
through,
Beside the river make for you
A tunnel of green gloom, and sleep
Deeply above; and green and deep
The stream mysterious glides beneath,
Green as a dream and deep as death.
-- Oh, damn! I know it! and I know
How the May fields all golden show,
And when the day is young and sweet,
Gild gloriously the bare feet
That run to bathe . . .

Ah God! to see the branches stir
Across the moon at Grantchester!
To smell the thrilling-sweet and rotten
Unforgettable, unforgotten
River-smell, and hear the breeze
Sobbing in the little trees.
Say, do the elm-clumps greatly stand
Still guardians of that holy land?
The chestnuts shade, in reverend dream,
The yet unacademic stream?
Is dawn a secret shy and cold
Anadyomene, silver-gold?
And sunset still a golden sea
From Haslingfield to Madingley?

59 Christina Harris
Appliqué and hand embroidery on dyed fabric

And after, ere the night is born,
Do hares come out about the corn?
Oh, is the water sweet and cool,
Gentle and brown, above the pool?
And laughs the immortal river still
Under the mill, under the mill?
Say, is there Beauty yet to find?
And Certainty? and Quiet kind?
Deep meadows yet, for to forget
The lies, and truths, and pain? . . . oh! yet
Stands the Church clock at ten to three?
And is there honey still for tea?

Rupert Brooke (1887 – 1915)

'Backward Glances' - Artists' Statements:

50 A Tent by Christopher Reid   **Artist Claire Benson**: "This poem vividly evokes a childhood experience. The tent, being made of fabric, lends itself to a realistic treatment in appliqué."

51 In Memoriam by Richard Stewart   **Artist Anne-Marie Stewart**: "I chose this poem because of a shared experience of destruction of beloved trees in the great gale, Autumn 1987."

52 Rock Me to Sleep by Elizabeth Allen   **Artist Hilary Sugai**: "The relentless passage of time waits for nothing and no-one.   If only we could go back just a little... but we cannot - so you must ENJOY EVERY DAY of your life: unable to recapture "moments", we must constantly make new ones."

53 Handbag by Ruth Fainlight   **Artist Hilary Burton**: "This poem had an instant appeal to me as I do have a very old handbag of my late mother's which has a distinct smell of make-up and leather. I also have my mother's collection of war time letters from my father, in the same condition as those described. Patchwork is my preferred needlework technique and I thought it might work well for a pictorial piece."

54 Handbag by Ruth Fainlight   **Artist Anne Reardon-James**: "This particular poem inspired fond memories of my Nan, who to this day continues to carry all her treasured possessions, photographs, indeed all of her life, in her handbag."

55 "Is my team ploughing ...." by A.E. Housman   **Artist Veronica Hall**: "Inspired by the awesome power of heavy horses, lines from Housman's poem suggested a team cleaving the land as they move across it. Furrows disappear under the ploughman striving to complete his work before the light fades."

56 In Flanders Fields by John McCrae   **Artist Elizabeth Brayshaw**: "Having had a father, and father-in-law, and also my husband serve in the British army, I have always been very aware of the great sacrifice made by young men in the cause of freedom. This poem is very emotive and the picture in my mind of the crosses and poppies lent itself well to the technique of appliqué."

57 The Little Dancers by Laurence Binyon   **Artist Jill Findlay**:   "In a few lines the poem draws the picture and conveys the atmosphere of the scene."

58 My Last Duchess by Robert Browning   **Artist Margaret Barraclough**:   "I was captivated by the intriguing story in this poem, and its dark undertones."

59 The Old Vicarage, Grantchester by Rupert Brooke
Artist Christina Harris: "There is a melancholy sadness in the poem, especially as the poet died three years later during World War 1. The last two lines are very well known and I wanted to show the aspects of the English countryside for which he is longing, so I tried to contrast these with the death and destruction which was to follow."

60 Patricia McLaughlin
Hand appliqué on hand dyed and painted fabric. Machine quilting

Windy Nights

Whenever the moon and stars are set,
    Whenever the wind is high,
All night long in the dark and wet,
    A man goes riding by.
Late in the night when the fires are out,
    Why does he gallop and gallop about?

Whenever the trees are crying aloud,
    And ships are tossed at sea,
By, on the highway, low and loud,
    By at the gallop goes he.
By at the gallop he goes, and then
    By he comes back at the gallop again.

R. L Stevenson (1850 – 1894)

Young at Heart

"A pocketful of yes's..."

Roger McGough

A sense of fun permeates the poems in this final section, including recollections of childhood poems that have endured even as the decades have passed, together with some celebrations of high-spirited nonsense.

Oberon's Feast (extract)

A little mushroom table spread,
After short prayers, they set on bread;
A moon-parched grain of purest wheat,
With some small glit'ring grit, to eat
His choice bits with; then in a trice
They make a feast less great than nice.
But all this while his eye is serv'd,
We must not think his ear was sterv'd:
But that there was in place to stir
His spleen, the chirring grasshopper,
The merry cricket, the puling fly,
The piping gnat for minstralcy.
And now, we must imagine first,
The elves present to quench his thirst
A pure seed-pearl of infant dew,
Brought and besweetened in a blue
And pregnant violet; which done
His kitling eyes begin to run
Quite through the table, where he spies
The horns of papery butterflies.

Robert Herrick (1591 – 1674)

61 Jill Hallett
Hand stitching and bead embellishment

On Midsummer's Eve

The night
  is hot
and still not
  dark
moths make
  circles
intent on
  the light.
Tonight
  we're told
the shy fairies
  show themselves
the elves
  will dance
round the magic
  ring.
What a wonderful
  thing!
Whether you
  believe in them
or not.

Ann Bonner

62 Angela Teasdale
Photo transfer with machine and hand stitching

The Cat and the Moon

The cat went here and there
And the moon spun round like a top,
And the nearest kin of the moon,
The creeping cat, looked up.
Black Minnaloushe stared at the moon,
For, wander and wail as he would,
The pure cold light in the sky
Troubled his animal blood.
Minnaloushe runs in the grass
Lifting his delicate feet.
Do you dance, Minnaloushe, do you dance?
When two close kindred meet,
What better than call a dance?
Maybe the moon may learn,
Tired of that courtly fashion,
A new dance turn.

Minnaloushe creeps through the grass
From moonlit place to place,
The sacred moon overhead
Has taken a new phase.
Does Minnaloushe know that his pupils
Will pass from change to change,
And that from round to crescent,
From crescent to round they range?
Minnaloushe creeps through the grass
Alone, important and wise,
And lifts to the changing moon
His changing eyes.

W.B. Yeats *(1865 – 1939)*

63 Jenny Jarvis
Machine stitching with appliqué, button and bead embellishment

Mary, Mary

Mary, Mary, quite contrary
How does your garden grow?
With silver bells
And cockleshells
And pretty maids all in a row.

Anon.

64 Cwmbran Tatters
Tatting on cotton and felt

The Pied Piper (extract)

65 Frances McArthur
Appliqué, hand and machine embroidery on painted fabrics

Into the street the Piper stepped,
Smiling first a little smile,
As if he knew what magic slept
In his quiet pipe the while;
Then, like a musical adept,
To blow the pipe his lips he wrinkled,
And green and blue his sharp eyes twinkled
Like a candle flame where salt is sprinkled;
And ere three shrill notes the pipe uttered,
You heard as if an army muttered;
And the muttering grew to a grumbling;
And the grumbling grew to a mighty rumbling;
And out of the houses the rats came tumbling.
Great rats, small rats, lean rats, brawny rats,
Brown rats, black rats, grey rats, tawny rats,
Grave old plodders, gay young friskers,
Fathers, mothers, uncles, cousins,
Cocking tails and pricking whiskers,
Families by tens and dozens,
Brothers, sisters, husbands, wives -
Followed the Piper for their lives.
From street to street he piped advancing,
And step for step they followed dancing,
Until they came to the river Weser,
Wherein all plunged and perished!

Robert Browning *(1812 – 1889)*

66 Jane O'Leary
Machine stitched with appliqué

Reward and Punishment

If you are very good, I will give you:

A pillow of blue strawberries
A swimming pool of Haagen Das
A mirror of imagination
A pocketful of yes's
A hiss of sleigh rides
A lunch box of swirling planets
A doorway of happy endings
A hedgerow of diamonds
A surfboard of dolphins
A cat's paw of tickles
A carton of fresh rainbow-juice
A forest of chocolate wardrobes

If you are naughty you will get:

A burst of balloon
A screech of wolf
A hoof of piggy bank
A twitch of sideways
A splinter of thirst
A precipice of banana skins
A tyrannosaurus of broccoli
A rucksack of bony elbows
A skeleton of lost pencils
A flag of inconvenience
A chill of false laughter
A blackboard of no way out

Roger McGough (1937 -   )

The Land of Counterpane

When I was sick and lay a-bed,
I had two pillows at my head,
And all my toys beside me lay,
To keep me happy all the day.

And sometimes for an hour or so
I watched my leaden soldiers go,
With different uniforms and drills,
Among the bed-clothes, through the hills;

And sometimes sent my ships in fleets
All up and down among the sheets;
Or brought my trees and houses out,
And planted cities all about.

I was the giant great and still
That sits upon the pillow-hill,
And sees before him, dale and plain,
The pleasant land of counterpane.

R. L Stevenson (1850 – 1894)

67 Kate Finlay
Machined fabric collage with hand embroidery

On the Ning Nang Nong

On the Ning Nang Nong
Where the Cows go Bong!
and the monkeys all say BOO!
There's a Nong Nang Ning
Where the trees go Ping!
And the tea pots jibber jabber joo.
On the Nong Ning Nang
All the mice go Clang
And you just can't catch 'em when they do!
So its Ning Nang Nong
Cows go Bong!
Nong Nang Ning
Trees go ping
Nong Ning Nang
The mice go Clang
What a noisy place to belong
is the Ning Nang Ning Nang Nong!!

Spike Milligan (1918 – 2002)

68 Gisburn Road County Primary School Year 3 Sewing Club
Felt appliqué and hand embroidery

69 Linda Connell
Appliqué, hand and machine quilting

Joy

A chatter of children
way up on Tennyson Down
hurtling into space they had found,
excitement dispersing mottled gulls,
bowled along on skittled legs
greeting the abundance of air.
Voices spiralling upward, kiteward
the day tilting them on
and beyond themselves.
Wind heckling their burning ears
snatching at clothes
grasping at hair
fingers spread and webbed
with blue, feet paddling
fast and faster,
swirls of laughter
scudding the sky
the joy of joys watching children fly.

Eve Jackson (1949 -   )

61

The Pig

It was an evening in November,
As I very well remember,
I was strolling down the street in drunken pride,
But my knees were all a-flutter,
And I landed in the gutter
And a pig came up and lay down by my side.

Yes, I lay there in the gutter
Thinking thoughts I could not utter,
When a colleen passing by did softly say
'You can tell a man who boozes
By the company he chooses' -
And the pig got up and slowly walked away.

Anon.

70 Claire Fell
Free Machine embroidery on hand dyed fabric

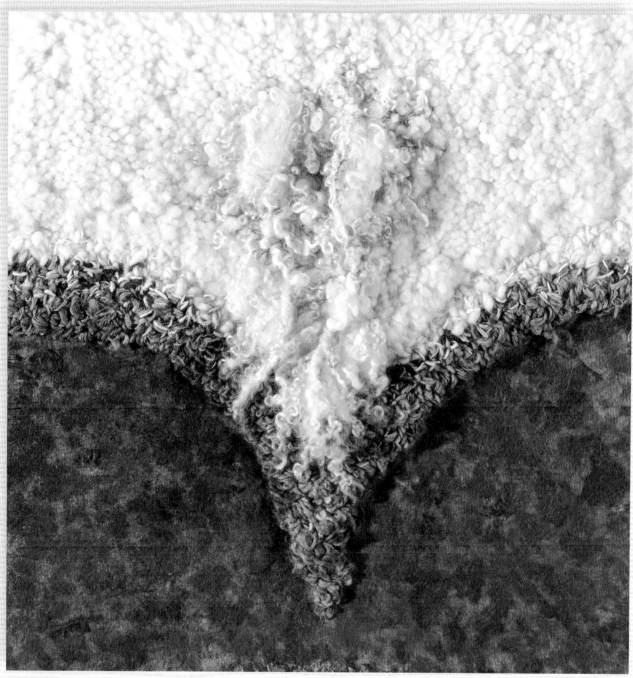

71 Susan Krekorian
Rug making techniques

Doormat

I am a doormat.
I'm brown and homespun
But my welcome's worn off.
I'm tired of taking it all lying down,
I bristle when I'm beaten.
Deep in the fibres of my being
I dream of becoming a thick-piled rug,
Fluffy and frivolous
On which seductions take place.
I'm going to let my hair down
So just watch your step.

Daphne Schiller (1942 -   )

'Young at Heart' - Artists' Statements:

60 Windy Nights by Robert Louis Stevenson **Artist Patricia McLaughlin**: "A favourite poem of my daughter when she was a child, this rekindled memories and presented me with the challenge of making a quilt to represent movement within a night scene."

61 Oberon's Feast by Robert Herrick **Artist Jill Hallett**: "For many years I have loved doing stumpwork, particularly insects, and this tied in well with this poem. I start with felt covered beads, cover them in silk, and hand embroider."

62 On Midsummer's Eve by Ann Bonner **Artist Angela Teasdale**: "I chose this poem because I believe in magic and fairies."

63 The Cat and The Moon by W.B. Yeats **Artist Jenny Jarvis**: "The idea for this particular piece came from watching my neighbour's cat, Charlie-cat as we call him, weaving down our garden, going through the hedge, over the wooden bridge where the evening primroses bloom in the evening light and striding across the fields into the distance. I have watched him do this many times and when the moon is full he is the cat who dances with the moon."

64 Mary, Mary, Quite Contrary Traditional **Artists Cwmbran Tatters**: "The group liked the pattern for a lady and the idea grew from this. All elements are tatted and represent the different levels of ability within the group."

65 The Pied Piper by Robert Browning **Artist Frances McArthur**: "I think I chose this poem because, although it is a children's poem, it has a dark message to it."

66 Reward and Punishment by Roger McGough **Artist Jane O'Leary**: "This was my daughter's favourite poem when she was five especially the line about a 'pocketful of yeses'. I saved her jeans so I could fill the pocket for her with a lifetime's worth of yeses."

67 The Land of Counterpane by Robert Louis Stevenson **Artist Kate Finlay**: "I have always liked this poem and believe it must have been based on Stevenson's own childhood experience. I have cut just under 300 pieces of fabric for this work!"

68 On The Ning Nang Nong by Spike Milligan **Artists Gisburn Road County Primary School Year 3 Sewing Club**: "We chose this poem because it gave us the opportunity to show lots of different stitches, especially after we simplified the 'picture' to noises and then chose stitches to match the noises."

69 Joy by Eve Jackson **Artist Linda Connell**: "This swirling windy poem made me think of kites flying on a cold day and children's sense of power, moving all those seagulls!"

70 The Pig by Anon. **Artist Claire Fell**: "The humour of the poem describes an uncomfortable moment for the male character. Judging by the colleen's disgust, he was probably too merry to notice! Appliqué suited the comedy of the poem and the machine embroidery helped define the detail and characterisation I wanted, whilst the painted elements tied the whole thing together so that the printed posters and signs did not look too out of place."

71 Doormat by Daphne Schiller **Artist Susan Krekorian**: "In the darkest hours of motherhood I can identify strongly with the sentiments of this poem; worn out and worn down by the ceaseless repetitive mundane demands. I long for acknowledgement that I am more than a domestic servant and for my fun, frivolous, creative and sensual self to be respected; so this is a self-portrait as a rug!"

Index

Pictures are numbered from No.1 at the beginning of the book

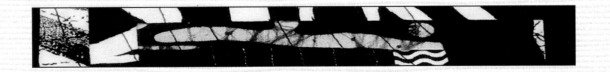